ULTIMATE 20

Supercars

Tracey Turner

EDGE
FRANKLIN WATTS

LONDON·SYDNEY

First published in 2013 by
Franklin Watts
338 Euston Road
London NW1 3BH

Franklin Watts Australia
Level 17/207 Kent Street
Sydney NSW 2000

Text © Tracey Turner 2013
Design © Franklin Watts 2013

Series editor: Adrian Cole
Art direction: Peter Scoulding
Design: D R Ink
Picture research: Diana Morris

Acknowledgements:
Aston Martin: 6. Brabus: 15. Bugatti: 4. Car Photo Library:
back cover t, 18, 19, 20, 21, 22. Dauer 962: 10. Gumpert: 16.
Nate Hawkbaker/CC/Wikipedia: title page. Hennessey: 7.
Koenigsegg: 9, 12. McLaren: front cover b, 13. 9ff: 8. Noble Cars: 17.
John Lamm/Transtock/Alamy: front cover t. Pagani: 23.
SSC North America: 5. Toastforbrekkie/CC. Wikimedia: 11.
Zenvo Automotive: 14.

Every attempt has been made to clear copyright.
Should there be any inadvertent omission please
apply to the publisher for rectification.

A CIP catalogue record for this book
is available from the British Library.

Dewey Classification: 629.2'221
ISBN: 978 1 4451 1446 0

Printed in China

Franklin Watts is a division of Hachette
Children's Books, an Hachette UK company.
www.hachette.co.uk

Warning! This is not a normal book!

Contents

Please note: every effort has been made by the Publishers to ensure
that the websites in this book contain no inappropriate or offensive
material. However, because of the nature of the Internet, it is impossible to
guarantee that the contents of these sites will not be altered. We strongly
advise that Internet access is supervised by a responsible adult.

Ultimate 20 is not just a book where you can find out loads of facts and stats about fantastic stuff – it's also a brilliant game book!

How to play

1. Grab a copy of *Ultimate 20* – oh, you have. OK, now get your friends to grab a copy, too.

2. Each player closes their eyes and flicks to a game page. Now, open your eyes and choose one of the Ultimate 20. Decide who goes first, then that person reads out what car they've chosen, plus the name of the stat. For example, this player has chosen the **McLaren P1** and the Price stat, with an Ultimate 20 ranking of 5.

Price: £800,000 (est.)	**5**
Top speed: 384 km/h (239 mph) (est.)	**9**
Engine capacity: 3,800 cc (est.)	**18**
Brake horsepower (bhp): 720 (est.)	**13**
0–100 (km/h): 2.9 seconds (est.)	**6**
Release date: 2013	**20**

3. Now, challenge your friends to see who has the highest-ranking stat – the lower the number (from 1–20) the better your chances of winning. (1 = good, 20 = goofy).

Player 1

Price: £800,000	**5**

Player 2

Price: £450,000	**11**

4. Whoever has the lowest number is the winner – nice one! If you have the same number – you've tied.

Time to flick, choose, challenge again!

(If you land on the same game page, choose the Ultimate 20 listing opposite.)

Mash it up!

If you haven't got the same *Ultimate 20* book as your friends, you can **STILL** play — Ultimate 20 **Mash Up!** The rules are the same as the regular game (above), so flick and choose one of your Ultimate 20 and a stat, then read out them out. Each player does this. Now read out the Ultimate 20 ranking to see whose choice is the best. Can Julius Caesar beat a werewolf? Can Bobby Charlton beat a king cobra snake?

Bugatti Veyron Super Sport

The Bugatti Veyron Super Sport is the fastest "legal" road car in the world. Its record-breaking top speed is powered by a 16-cylinder engine with four turbochargers, which gulps air from cooling ducts set into the roof.

Sleek and powerful

The shape of the Bugatti Veyron Super Sport – long and low – is not simply designed to attract attention as you drive past. No, the sleek shape cuts through the air for higher speeds. Most of the body is built from carbon fibre, instead of metal. Carbon fibre is very lightweight so less power is needed to move the car, allowing it to travel faster.

Price: £1.7 million *1*
Top speed: 431 km/h (267 mph) *3*
Engine capacity: 7,993 cc *3*
Brake horsepower (bhp): 1,200 *3*
0–100 (km/h): 2.5 seconds *1*
Release date: 2010
13

Famous names

- Bugatti was a famous car manufacturer in the early twentieth century. The Volkswagen Group bought the brand and began designing and building Bugatti supercars in 1998.

- The Veyron, which was first developed in 2005, is named after a French Grand Prix racing driver called Pierre Veyron. He raced Bugatti cars during the 1930s, 40s and 50s.

SSC Ultimate Aero TT

The SSC Ultimate Aero TT held the record for the fastest road car in the world from 2007 to 2010, when the record was broken by the Bugatti Veyron Super Sport. The "TT" stands for the car's twin-turbocharged engine.

Aero design

This car is designed to be highly aerodynamic — Ultimate Aero, get it? The engine is at the rear of the car, so that the front can be lower to make the air flow over it more smoothly. During its development, the car was actually tested at a wind tunnel belonging to NASA. That's where the US space organisation tests rockets. Whoosh!

Tuatara record hopes

SSC North America, the US-based company that makes the Ultimate Aero, hopes to regain the world record with its SSC Tuatara, launched in 2013. The Tuatara is named after a type of lizard from New Zealand, which, apparently, is evolving faster than any other animal in the world.

Price: £405,662   **12**

Top speed: 413 km/h (257 mph)   **5**

Engine capacity: 6,200 cc   **8**

Brake horsepower (bhp): 1,287   **1**

0–100 (km/h): 2.7 seconds   **4**

Release date: 2007   **9**

Aston Martin One-77

The beautifully streamlined Aston Martin One-77 is one of the best looking cars in the world. Its styling is in keeping with Aston Martin tradition, featuring a massive grille on the front.

Million-pound style

There's a limited edition of 77 of these supercars, so each One-77 is one of 77. That's where the name comes from (it was obvious, right?) Your £1,200,000 pays for a hand-built, mostly carbon fibre body, and a powerful V12 engine. The One-77's elegant styling has won a bucket load of design awards. But, don't break open your piggy bank just yet, because all 77 cars have been sold.

Price: £1.2 million — 2

Top speed: 354 km/h (220 mph) — 16

Engine capacity: 7312 cc — 2

Brake horsepower (bhp): 750 — 10

0–100 (km/h): 3.7 seconds — 18

Release date: 2008 — 10

The name's Bond

- British company Aston Martin is one of the world's most famous luxury car brands.

- Aston Martin cars have featured in six James Bond movies, complete with ejector seats, missiles, lasers, machine-guns and cloaking devices.

Hennessey Venom GT

Only six Hennessey Venom GT cars exist so far: they were made to order for those who could afford the price tag. The manufacturer of the Hennessey Venom GT says it is capable of 437 km/h – but this top speed has never been tested. No other road car this lightweight is capable of this sort of speed.

UK and USA

The cars are built using the modified body of a lightweight British sports car: the Lotus Exige. The 6.2-litre, LS9 V8 engine is built in the USA by General Motors. The engine and the body are put together, and the cars tested, at Silverstone, England.

Under control

The driver can adjust the twin turbochargers to provide different levels of boost. There is also an automatic aero wing on the back which helps to stabilise the car.

Golden engine

The Hennessey Venom has 24-carat gold-leaf heat shields in its engine. Gold is also used in spacecraft because it is good at reflecting heat and light.

Price: £681,890 — 8

Top speed: 437 km/h (272 mph) (claimed) — 2

Engine capacity: 6,200 cc — 8

Brake horsepower (bhp): 1,244 — 2

0–100 (km/h): 2.5 seconds — 1

Release date: 2010 — 13

9ff GT9-R

The 9ff GT9-R is made by German car tuning company 9ff, which specialises in converting Porsche cars into race cars that are also legal to drive on ordinary roads. The company holds records for top speed for a car powered by alternative fuel, and top speed for a convertible car.

911 to 9ff

The 9ff GT9-R is based on a Porsche 911 GT3, but it is heavily modified. Unlike almost all Porsches, which have their engines in the rear of the car, the GT9-R is mid-engined. This helps to distribute weight more evenly. The engine has been modified from a 911 Turbo to provide a huge amount of power and speed. Four engines exploded during tests to find the right kind of coating for the engine's cylinders. Boom!

Small, medium or large?

The car is available with three different levels of power, ranging from 750 bhp to 1,120 bhp. Customers can also choose from three different gearboxes, as well as different aerodynamic features.

Price: £540,000 — 9

Top speed: 414 km/h (256 mph) — 4

Engine capacity: 4,000 cc — 17

Brake horsepower (bhp): 1,120 — 4

0–100 (km/h): 2.9 seconds — 6

Release date: 2009 — 11

Koenigsegg Agera R

The Koenigsegg Agera R holds the Guinness World Record for the fastest time from 0–300 km/h: 21.19 seconds. That's similar to a passenger aircraft speeding along the runway before take-off.

Different by design

The Koenigsegg Agera R has a sleek carbon fibre body and a powerful 5-litre engine. The car has a unique design: the hard top comes off and can be stowed underneath the bonnet, while the doors open forward and to the side. Koenigsegg call this – are you ready, take a deep breath – the dihedral synchro-helix actuation system.

Price: £1 million — 3

Top speed: 440 km/h (272 mph) (claimed) — 1

Engine capacity: 5,000 cc — 12

Brake horsepower (bhp): 1,100 — 6

0–100 (km/h): 2.9 seconds — 6

Release date: 2011 — 16

Swedish supercars

Koenigsegg is a Swedish company founded in 1994 by Christian Koenigsegg. The company only makes supercars. It's the only car manufacturer to have two cars in the Ultimate 20.

Dauer 962 LM

The Dauer 962's initials "LM" stand for Le Mans, where the famous endurance sports car race is held in France. In 1994, a racing version of the Dauer 962 LM won at Le Mans.

Price: £750,000 6

Top speed: 404 km/h (251.4 mph) 6

Engine capacity: 2,994 cc 20

Brake horsepower (bhp): 730 12

0–100 (km/h): 2.6 seconds 3

Release date: 1993 2

Converted Porsche

The Dauer 962 LM is based on the Porsche 962 racing car. Dauer adapted the 962 LM so it could be driven on ordinary roads. These changes included building a new carbon fibre and Kevlar® body, adding a second seat and changing the suspension system to meet height requirements for street cars. However, the engine is almost the same as the racing version.

Limited edition

All Dauer 962s were made from Porsche 962s that had actually raced, so not very many were made. The exact number remains a secret, but there are probably fewer than fifteen cars altogether. The super-rich Sultan of Brunei owns six of them!

Porsche at Le Mans

The road circuit at Le Mans is 13.65 km long, and is one of the oldest and fastest in the world. Porsche is the most successful maker of Le Mans race cars, with sixteen victories. Drivers Hans Hermann and Richard Attwood won the first overall victory for Porsche in 1970.

Saleen S7 Twin Turbo

The US-made Saleen S7 Twin Turbo is an updated version of the Saleen S7. The S7 had an 8-cylinder engine capable of 550 bhp, but with the addition of twin turbochargers in the new version, Saleen increased this to a blistering 750 bhp.

Upside down

The twin turbochargers are fitted to the Saleen S7 TT's engine – a Ford 427, 7-litre V8. The car has new front and rear diffusers, and a rear spoiler. This gives the car greater downforce, helping it to grip the road. In theory, at a speed of 257 km/h, the car creates a downward pressure that's equal to its weight. That means it could be driven upside down, on the roof of a tunnel. No one has tried this out – so far!

Racing S7

There is a racing version of the S7, the S7R. It won the famous endurance race, the 24 Hours of Le Mans, in 2010.

Price: £345,000	16
Top speed: 399 km/h (248mph)	7
Engine capacity: 6,991 cc	5
Brake horsepower (bhp): 750	10
0–100 (km/h): 3.2 seconds	14
Release date: 2005	4

Koenigsegg CCX

The Koenigsegg CCX is the second car from this Swedish manufacturer to make the Ultimate 20. It was made five years before the Koenigsegg Agera R. The CCX has a 4.7-litre, 8-cylinder, supercharged engine capable of speeds approaching 400 km/h.

Green features

The Koenigsegg CCX was the first road car to use carbon fibre wheels, which are much lighter than the alloy wheels found on many supercars. A new version of the car, the Koenigsegg CCXR, was released in 2008. It can run on biofuel as well as ordinary petrol, making it more environmentally friendly.

Price: £405,000	13
Top speed: 395 km/h (245 mph)	8
Engine capacity: 4,700 cc	14
Brake horsepower (bhp): 806	8
0–100 (km/h): 3.2 seconds	14
Release date: 2006	6

Top Gear test

"The Stig", the driver for the TV programme *Top Gear*, spun a Koenigsegg CCX off the test track in 2008. A rear spoiler was added to the car, and the Stig successfully completed the test lap. It became the fastest time recorded on the show at the time.

McLaren P1

Back in the 1990s, the McLaren F1 was the fastest road car in the world. Now, McLaren have introduced its successor, the McLaren P1, the most eagerly awaited new supercar of recent years.

P1 design

McLaren have used clever innovations to make the McLaren P1 as light as possible: as well as carbon fibre, the car uses aluminium panels, special brakes and super light wheels. The unusual door ducts, an eye-catching feature, draw air into the car's cooling system to keep its massive engine cool.

Price: £800,000 (est.) — **5**

Top speed: 384 km/h (239 mph) (est.) — **9**

Engine capacity: 3,800 cc (est.) — **18**

Brake horsepower (bhp): 720 (est.) — **13**

0–100 (km/h): 2.9 seconds (est.) — **6**

Release date: 2013 — **20**

Made by McLaren

- McLaren Racing has been racing cars since 1963.
- McLaren Racing is one of the most successful racing teams in Formula 1 Grand Prix motor racing.
- McLaren Automotive has been manufacturing supercars since 1989.

Zenvo ST1

The Zenvo ST1 is the world's only Danish supercar, and is built entirely in Denmark. It has a supercharged, 7-litre V8 turbocharged engine. The company's founders wanted to make a beautifully designed supercar that was suitable for everyday use, as well as for driving at speed. Imagine being dropped off at school in this!

Small, light and fast

The Zenvo ST1 is small, light and streamlined, with a steel frame and carbon fibre body panels. The engine was exclusively designed by Zenvo, rather than using an existing engine as many supercars do. Only fifteen Zenvo ST1s are made per year, at a cost of £750,000 each.

In-car features

The car has three driving modes: wet, sport and race. These change the engine output depending on the desired driving experience. In race mode, the car delivers 1,104 bhp. The car also has a keyless entry system and a head-up display.

Price: £750,000	6
Top speed: 375 km/h (232 mph)	10
Engine capacity: 7,000 cc	4
Brake horsepower (bhp): 1,104	5
0–100 (km/h): 3 seconds	9
Release date: 2009	11

Brabus Rocket 800

Brabus is a German car tuning company, which specialises in modifying Mercedes-Benz cars. The Brabus Rocket 800 is based on the Mercedes CLS generation of cars. It's the fastest saloon car (a passenger car with two rows of seats) in the world. It's the only Ultimate 20 supercar that has four doors.

Price: £345,000   **16**
Top speed: 367 km/h (227 mph)   **12**
Engine capacity: 6,300 cc   **7**
Brake horsepower (bhp): 788   **9**
0–100 (km/h): 3.7 seconds   **18**
Release date: 2012   **19**

Rocket power

The Brabus Rocket 800 is powered by a 12-cylinder, 6.3-litre engine. It's modified from the engine of a 600 series Mercedes, with increased capacity to give it greater horsepower. The "800" refers to the amount of horsepower the car generates. Although it is capable of higher speeds, the car is limited to 349 km/h for road driving.

Brabus history

Brabus started performing high-performance modifications in 1977. Based in Germany, it redesigns Mercedes-AMG engines, and makes other changes, including adding spoilers and bodykits, and upgrading exhaust systems and brakes.

Gumpert Apollo

The Gumpert Apollo is powered by a twin-turbo Audi V8. Its eye-catching design (which some people love, and others hate) includes large air intakes on the front and sides that feed air to the brakes and turbochargers.

Price: £210,000	18
Top speed: 360 km/h (223 mph)	15
Engine capacity: 4,163 cc	16
Brake horsepower (bhp): 650	17
0–100 (km/h): 3.1 seconds	12
Release date: 2005	4

Enraged Apollos

Roland Gumpert, a former Audi engineer, set up the Gumpert company in 2004. He named his supercar design "Apollo" after the ancient Greek and Roman god of the Sun. In 2012, two new Apollos were unveiled: a racing version, and a supercar called Apollo Enraged, which is more powerful at 780bhp. Only three Apollo Enraged cars will be made.

Making an entrance

Getting in and out of a Gumpert Apollo can be tricky: it has gull-wing doors. The driver and passenger have to climb in, but at least the driver can remove the steering wheel to make things a bit easier!

Noble M600

The Noble M600 is manufactured by Noble Autocars in Leicester, England. Only 50 of the supercars are made every year, powered by a twin-turbocharged Volvo V8 engine.

Computer unaided

The Noble company was bought in 2006 by Peter Dyson, who'd noticed that the cars he liked driving best were the ones with less computer-aided features. The aim of the Noble M600 was to make a car that didn't rely as heavily on computer assistance as most modern supercars do.

No extras

The Noble M600 comes without an anti-lock braking system (ABS) or automatic stabilisation management (ASM). This means the car relies more on the skill of the driver to keep it under control.

Carbon body

A full carbon fibre body (shown below) reduces the car's weight to just 1,250 kg – the same as a large female walrus!

Price: £200,000 — **20**

Top speed: 362 km/h (225 mph) — **13**

Engine capacity: 4,439 cc — **15**

Brake horsepower (bhp): 650 — **17**

0–100 (km/h): 3 seconds — **9**

Release date: 2010 — **13**

Bristol Fighter T

The Bristol Fighter has been made by British company
Bristol Cars since 2004. In 2006, the Fighter T was launched –
a turbocharged version of the Bristol Fighter.

Bristol Cars

- Bristol Cars has been trading since the 1940s.
- Its classic 1950s and 60s models have star owners, including Sir Richard Branson and Liam Gallagher.
- It's a secretive company – it has just one showroom, in London, and won't tell anyone how many Bristol Fighters have been made – not even Ultimate 20!

Extreme engine

The Bristol Fighter T's front-mounted engine
is enormous: 10 cylinders, with a capacity of
nearly 8 litres. It's based on a Chrysler engine,
and has been modified to generate 1012 bhp.
The car's top speed is limited to 362 km/h
(fast enough for most people), but some
sources claim it is capable of 434 km/h.

Price: £352,000 — 14
Top speed: 362 km/h (225 mph) — 13
Engine capacity: 7,994 cc — 1
Brake horsepower (bhp): 1,012 — 7
0–100 (km/h): 3.5 seconds — 17
Release date: 2006 — 6

Ascari A10

The Ascari A10 is based on a racing car also made by British company Ascari – the KZ1-R GT. Both cars were designed by Paul Brown, who used to design Formula 1 racing cars.

Price: £350,000

Top speed: 354 km/h (220 mph)

Engine capacity: 4,941 cc

Brake horsepower (bhp): 625

0–100 (km/h): 2.8 seconds

Release date: 2006

15
16
13
19
5
6

OU55 GWJ

Racing power

The A10 has a carbon fibre body and is powered by a 5-litre BMW V8 engine. If you were expecting a comfortable interior, then you might be in for a shock. There's no air conditioning, no soundproofing and there isn't even a stereo! No more than 50 Ascari A10s were built, and each one was crafted by hand.

Famous name

Ascari was founded in England by Klaas Zwart, a Dutch billionaire, in 1995. It's named after Italian racing car driver Alberto Ascari, who raced during the 1940s and 50s. He was the first driver to win the Formula 1 championship twice. The "A10" got its name because it was launched during the company's tenth anniversary.

Ferrari Enzo

Ferrari is probably the most famous car manufacturer and racing team in the world. The Enzo is named after Enzo Ferrari, the Italian racing driver of the 1920s and 1930s. He started the company in 1947.

Inspiring a generation

The Enzo is powered by a Ferrari F140 V12 engine, and features a carbon fibre and aluminium body. Its aerodynamic design was inspired by Ferrari Formula 1 cars. Some say it's the ugliest Ferrari ever made!

High demand

Just 400 Enzos were made between 2002–2004. The car is in such demand that every time one of them crashes, the value of the others goes up. The cost of a used Ferrari Enzo is over half a million pounds.

Price: £450,000 — 11

Top speed: 350 km/h (217 mph) — 18

Engine capacity: 5,988 cc — 11

Brake horsepower (bhp): 660 — 16

0–100 (km/h): 3.1 seconds — 12

Release date: 2002 — 3

Jaguar XJ220

The XJ220 was Jaguar's first production supercar. It was the world's fastest road car from 1992 until the McLaren F1 beat the world record in 1994.

K644 WJO

High-speed handling

The XJ220 proved popular, partly due to its excellent handling. The car was one of the first road cars to maximise downforce, so that the car "stuck" to the road even at very high speeds. As well as its fastest road car record, held until 1994, the XJ220 also held the Nürburgring production car lap record until 2000.

Price: £460,000 — 10
Top speed: 350 km/h (217 mph) — 18
Engine capacity: 3,498 cc — 19
Brake horsepower (bhp): 542 — 20
0–100 (km/h): 3.9 seconds — 20
Release date: 1992 — 1

Jaguar brand

Founded in 1922, Jaguar is one of the oldest and most famous British car brands (though it's now owned by Indian company, Tata Motors). Jaguar was originally called the Swallow Sidecar Company, but changed its name after World War II to avoid sharing initials with the SS, a Nazi military unit.

Lamborghini Aventador

Lamborghini is one of the most famous supercar brands in the world. The Aventador is Lamborghini's top model.

Aventador the Bull

The name of the car makes reference to Lamborghini's logo, a fighting bull – ¡Olé! Aventador was the name of an especially courageous prize-winning Spanish fighting bull. The car's body is made completely from carbon fibre. The 12-cylinder, 6.5-litre V12 engine is made using a lightweight aluminium-silicon alloy for everything except the most heat-exposed parts.

Price: £201,900   19
Top speed: 350 km/h (217 mph)   18
Engine capacity: 6,498 cc   6
Brake horsepower (bhp): 690   15
0–100 (km/h): 2.9 seconds   6
Release date: 2011   16

Aventador J

There's a limited production of 4,000 Aventadors, for which there's a waiting list, but only one Aventador J has been made. It has no roof or windscreen and the driver has to have special equipment in order to drive it at speeds over 300 km/h. It sold for £1.7 million.

Pagani Huayra

Italian car manufacturer Pagani released the Huayra (say "Wai-y-ra") following the huge success of its Zonda supercars. It's named after a South American god of the wind – and you might have to be a god to afford it!

Carbon-titanium

Pagani developed a new material for its Zonda which is also used on the Huayra. Its body is made of carbon-titanium, which makes the car extremely strong, yet lightweight. In fact, at just 1,350 kg it's one of the lightest supercars.

Active aerodynamics

The Huayra's aerodynamics change according to driving conditions: the height of the car from the ground, and four aerodynamic flaps on the front and rear of the car are able to alter depending on speed, acceleration and steering angle.

Price: £1 million **3**
Top speed: 370 km/h (229 mph) **11**
Engine capacity: 5.980 cc **10**
Brake horsepower (bhp): 720 **13**
0–100 (km/h): 3.3 seconds **16**
Release date: 2011 **16**

Glossary

4/5/6/7-litre engine – a measurement of the internal size of an engine

8/10/12/16-cylinder engine – an engine with a certain number of cylinders; the parts of the engine where fuel is burned to generate power

aerodynamic – having a shape that reduces the drag from air moving past, allowing the car to move more swiftly

biofuel – a fuel derived from living material, such as rapeseed, soya beans, sugar cane or maize

car tuning – improving the performance or appearance of a car

carbon fibre – an extremely strong, lightweight material

convertible – a car with a folding or canvas roof

downforce – downward pressure which helps a car hold the road

evolving – developing over time, especially an animal changing over generations

gull-wing doors – car doors that are hinged at the roof and open straight up – they look like wings

handling – how a car holds the road and how it feels to drive it

streamlined – describes a shape that provides little air resistance

suspension system – a mechanical system of springs or shock absorbers connecting the wheel axis to the body of the car

turbochargers – these give a car engine up to 50 per cent more power by pushing more fuel and air into the existing cylinders in the engine

Index